May Day

POEMS

Gretchen Marquette

Graywolf Press

This publication is made possible, in part, by the voters of Minnesota through a Minnesota State Arts Board Operating Support grant, thanks to a legislative appropriation from the arts and cultural heritage fund, and through grants from the National Endowment for the Arts and the Wells Fargo Foundation Minnesota. Significant support has also been provided by the Jerome Foundation, Target, the McKnight Foundation, the Amazon Literary Partnership, and other generous contributions from foundations, corporations, and individuals. To these organizations and individuals we offer our heartfelt thanks.

Published by Graywolf Press
250 Third Avenue North, Suite 600
Minneapolis, Minnesota 55401

www.graywolfpress.org

Published in the United States of America

ISBN 978-1-55597-739-9

2 4 6 8 9 7 5 3 1
First Graywolf Printing, 2016

Library of Congress Control Number: 2015953602

Cover design: Jeenee Lee Design

Cover art: Eamonn McLain, "34th and 15th," from the series *Around the Park.* 2014. Oil pastel relief on spray-painted wood. Used with the permission of the artist. Digital image created by Nikki Ivanovsky-Schow.

FOR BRIDGET

FOR MY FRIENDS

Contents

I

II

III

IV

V

For nothing can be sole or whole / That has not been rent.

—W. B. YEATS

May Day

I

Elsewhere

I've kept it quiet,
where to find the brightest,
most exacting love.
Much of it burns off.

What remains, remains.

Fox-wild, desire
is a trap. I recognize
places I've slept

despite every branch broken
and the new snow.
What I said before, about love,
you have to let it be.

I've never told
how I walk around thinking
of the hollow of a throat or curve
of a shoulder or how I hold the reins
of horses who are men in hiding.

We sat under hot light,
in a round room plush with the breath
of strangers. I said, *We have
seventy pages left to love one another.*
Across his chest burst a sash
of gold chrysanthemum.

One thing I've learned—
you have to let love be practice
for what might happen

elsewhere.

Doe

A Wounded Deer—leaps highest—
EMILY DICKINSON

The smell of wet,
like earth, like the breath
of the beloved.
There's movement

on the opposite side
of the wall, a deer, head
down, licking at a shallow
wound. I hope you know

how hard this is, to arrive,
to remember the way in.
I have dreams I return home,
find everything changed,

and I'm lost in hallways,
between walls. I hear birds,
though I don't know what sort.
They serve no poetic function,

but they sing. Think of them
as wild birds, use any image
that comes to mind. I imagine
small scraps of tissue: red

and blue and green—not birds,
but moving like them, and singing.
The doe lifts her head. Sometimes
the deer has a split

ear. Sometimes the doe
is made of bone, the femur
warped, broken and healed.
How would it be, to lie

in wet grass, or snow,
leg broken—to need water, to get up
again? Don't think on it too long.
I know I'd die of thirst.

During Thanksgiving dinner,
everyone laughed at his story,
how he'd shot a buck with six points,
found it was a doe, a doe with antlers.

Why are so many love stories tragedies?

Prologue

There was a child carried
into the house after a long
drive. Aware of the *hush*
hush noise of father's feet
on the carpet, she felt
for the first time her weight
in someone else's arms.

Know Me

I was once the tree you hammered shims into
so you could climb me like a ladder.

And I was the new strawberry, larvae white and hard,
and the bleeding-heart bush dropping valentines over your acreage.

I was the fox on whom you did not pull the trigger, the air trapped
beneath the frozen creek, and the broken milkweed's white sap.

I did my growing far from you, arrived
late one summer, shirt like a tartan flag.

Come over. I said. *Get to know me.*

Now I am the bottle-blue boat, lost in the squall of you,
and the wave curling over your head.

Prophecy

You will bruise the meat of your palm
striking the wall, open handed,
trying to quiet squirrels gnawing
behind plaster, inches away
but out of reach. You will have lived
for months, on milk and oranges,
the result being a sweet mouth.
This is the day you'll come home
to your spare keys naked
and singular unto themselves—
teeth set on edge as you touch the first one,
cold on the table, find the other, hidden
under the door, locked from outside.

Your sleeping body will be protected
by a bolt of metal, your sleeping body
will be full of raw sugar
and milk fat. But first you will lie
awake, pressing the bruised palm.
You will have a quiet mouth, untasted.
You'll have the sound of teeth
grinding red wire. You'll have the sound
a woman makes. You'll have no trouble imagining
the key thrust into the lock, *shock*—and then
the turning, *slick*. You'll believe you want
a recording of it—the last sound
he made in your life.

Colossus

On the outskirts of town,
past the seven churches
and eleven bars. Past the yellow
bungalow of the woman
who sold pumpkins.

Past the yard with the white
ducks. Away from the horses,
heads down, talking to the grass.
Past the field where Tom and I
flew our kite. Over the blue bridge.

Past the ice-cream parlor and its rainbow
sherbet. Past the post office and defunct
theater's permanent red-letter marquee.
Past the library's picture books
and white squirrel under her bell jar.

Past Shepard's hamburger stand. Away
from the smell of the paper mill
and color of the river. To the place
where lines were painted on the center lane.
Past the liquor store, and the ramshackle

house of the couple who'd lost their only child.
To where the ditches got deep. I'd beg them
to take me outside of town where the giant
buck lived. I could spot him from a distance—
he was a hundred feet tall, antlers regal

and chalk white. He watched us arrive
from the field near the gravel lot. Up close,
you couldn't see him anymore
in his static, frozen jump. The paint
on his body was chipped, spattered

by birds. If you patted him, there was an empty
sound. I always wanted to be taken to him,
but the closer I drew, the more it was snuffed out—
what burned in my chest.

Gregory

(West Point)

Traveling those dark roads to see him, twisting
through carved forests, the eyes of animals

appeared jewel bright in the sweep
of my headlights. He didn't want to pose

for pictures, hot in his dress gray-over-whites,
the coat with the bullet buttons, all of us

sweating as we pointed out statues
he'd strode by thousands of times. I kept mistaking

another girl's brother for him, marching in formation,
soft haircuts under plumes of black feathers.

He was already less ours. Later,
in blue jeans, he skipped rocks on the Hudson,

the river swallowing the sun in a rush, boats
scattering across the long arm of the water,

tiny lights I would remember
when I fastened a bracelet to my wrist,

spectrum of stones, he gave me for Christmas
when he was twelve.

Andromeda

From 150,000,000,000,000,000,000 miles away,
they took Andromeda's photograph, tinted it like a daguerreotype,
put her in a purple dress. We've got Hubble, got the electron microscope.
You can choose between them but still see the same thing. Almost 500,
000,000,000,000,000,000,000 atoms in a teaspoon
of water.

A star exploded, bore iron,
then came blood. The hole in my jaw has clotted
with something from a star. Lost tooth, too weak to last
my lifetime, it will exist, broken and bad, long after my femurs
turn carbon. This transmutation—it's how my beloved will become
an olive tree, an eggshell. There are places in the universe where time matters
less. Remember this when you want to gut yourself, in love with a married or dead man.
If you can figure how to try again, you could be the one fixing your hair for him,
be the one he'll probably stop loving. You still have a chance to meet the other
one, some afternoon at the piano, a duet. *The dark magnolia of your belly,*
when you sense it and tremble, you can be a wave of salt water,
you can collapse for a little while. Time matters less,
in other places in the universe. Fetus, mummy,
think about all that new skin.

And think about your body
and its toughness, how briefly it's allowed
to be. You've got to see it through. Glut yourself
with the sound of bells if you have to, use whatever you need.
It's such a fleeting state really, like the sixty-second theatrical tour
of Andromeda, flushed in red and gold. A body, heavenly or not. Her name
means *to think of a man*. Andromeda, reserved for one she didn't love, chained to a rock,
doomed to be devoured. She still had passion, seven sons, a little girl, heavenly
entombment—but believe me, you may never get what you want. So when
your ribs prove too small a cage for such feeling, bones bowing outward,
and higher up, you're almost blind, you can stand still, you can be
a conductor. You can think of a cluster of stars, you can think
of one of your atoms as a galaxy with its own type
of horse, and music, maybe something akin to
the viola. There are mothers there, certainly,
and something like the vulture.

Think of a woman, wrists manacled,
think of any Nautilus shell, of any name you've given,
it may as well have been Andromeda. We may be laying this place to waste
and you may never get what you want. It can't matter much.
Somewhere a star is ceasing to be a star.
We call it death.

Painted Turtle

Summer road the ring around the lake, we drove mostly in silence.

Why aren't I your wife?

You swerved around a turtle sunning itself.

I wanted to go back. To hold the hot disc of it and place it in the grass.

We were late for dinner.

One twentieth of a mile an hour, I said. *Claws in tar.* You turned the car around.

Traffic from the direction of the turtle, and you saw before I did, the fifty bones of the carapace,

crushed Roman dome, the surprise of red blood.

I couldn't help crying, couldn't keep anything from harm.

I'm sorry, you said, and let it hurt.

The relief, always, of you in the seat beside me, you'll never know.

Driving that road next winter, you remembered that place in the road. *Your turtle.*

During hibernation, a turtle's heart beats once for every ten minutes.

It cannot voluntarily open its eyes.

Macrocosm/Microcosm

Horses are pulling grass
with their square teeth—
their hollow throats
sweeten their chest cavities.
I can go weeks without thinking of whales
and they never think of me. One pair
of human eyes first saw
the planet Saturn. Where are the bones
of the dog I loved first?
Which are the trees
that will become invitations?

Somewhere, a dish sits in a sink
holding only three crumbs and
I will never eat from this dish
no matter how hungry
I become. How long has it been
since I've considered the leopard,
its fire growing smaller
in the jungle hearth?
Filaments are bursting
inside bulbs. Oranges are falling,
dully, from branches. Plants everywhere
are laying down their green planks.

Either the man who will kill
my brother does not exist,
or else he has been breathing for decades
under the Iraqi sun.

I Know One Thing for Sure

I was born first. Birds nested in the eaves of our house. I didn't find new birds ugly. I liked seeing blood in their naked bellies, like the veins in my skin, like the blue line in the night crawler, wet in the ground. I wasn't allowed to watch storms come through. I remained in the basement under the pulse of the siren, frustrated. I always wanted to touch the soft muzzles of horses, grazing in the fields. Sometimes I was allowed. *Hold your hand flat,* they said.

I was born first. My sister came later, blue eyed and girl soft. When I was small, a dog bit my face; I could've lost an eye but the tooth found my cheekbone instead. Bone against bone.

I was born first. My brother came along later. It was coming on Christmas. The lights were what mattered, lights of every color. My brother was small and red. My brother was like an animal, warm and murmuring. My brother was like an animal and I loved him that way. I'd been in the hospital for surgery the week before his birth. I woke at midnight to the blue light of the television, my pregnant mother asleep in a chair. Everything hurt. I have been close to death, but not enough to know it well; it's been like flying over the desert in a plane. I remember one night, the gentle pressure of the boy's fingers, finding the bones of my face and skull—*mandible, maxilla*—when he finished, I said *again,* the way a child does, and he traced the sockets of my closed eyes.

I was born first. I want my own child now. I want him to place his hands on either side of my ribcage and make me feel small again. I want to feel the burst of his breath against my neck, just below my ear, the way he breathes when he first finds the part of me he most wants to touch. The damp center. The dying star. Sitting in the dark of the restaurant, leaning forward to hear you, face over a tea light, hands cupped over my ears under my hair, I couldn't understand how a person's eyes could be that dark and still be blue. Or how wicked affection is, once you've let it loose.

II

Deer Suite

And these deer at my bramble gate: so close
here, we touch our own kind in each other.

                                        TU FU

(I)

Her neighbor was an archer who drew his bow
on paper deer.

He tacked them to trees in the ecotone between
his clipped lawn

and the scrolling ferns and roots
of the woods.

Told to stay back, she went close enough
to hear arrows

shuck and plait light between birches, to listen
to the piercing

of their paper lungs. The deer stood,
arrow filled,

eyes trained on the horizon. Dusk
masked their falseness.

(II)

At school we dissected the hearts
of deer, gifts

from hunters, our fathers.
Hearts frozen

and thawed, glistening on blue dissection
mats. They reeked.

It was the stink of old death. But how
did we know? We knew.

We looked at one another, pretended
we didn't want to pull

our scalpels along ventricles, the hair
on our arms stiff

and no spit in our mouths. It wasn't
like the sheep's eye,

or the pitiable frog, pithed for us
out of sight.

Blood implied a living thing. All
that remained was

its four-chambered heart.

(III)

They asked us to envision medieval surgeon
William Harvey

standing over the living doe belted
to his table. We tried

to imagine the thrill of discovery
at her open chest,

the way ventricles sucked his fingers
like women

or infants did. He named the domed
structures atriums: rooms

filled with light. But we were thinking
about heat,

what the doe's body transferred
to his hand, the tarry dark

of her blood. The hearts we opened
held thickets of clots, pearls

of blood like blueberries from a tin,
lumps like buckshot.

(IV)

If I say my longing is a doe,
that it bounds,

that it chokes, has parts that splinter,
that it can be split

from breastbone to pelvis. If I tell you
I remember the doe,

strung up in the neighbor's yard, throat
unzipped, flesh

delivered again in a surge of water,
that I'd never seen anything

born; calves came at night, but deer
were butchered

during daylight. If I tell how I watched
her dismantled,

that I searched for the deer
in the hide like a pit

in a plum. That he plundered her
but I found nothing there.

If I say the rope was stained copper yellow.
That it became the color

of ruin under the green walnut tree.
If I say that it had a scent

like rain in rusted eaves, will you
tell me, then?

When the deer leave after dusk,
where do they go?

Trophy

Up north, deer are eye lights among pines,
green lanterns of *tapeta lucida,* ghosts
licking the salty periphery of dreams.
They're tabletop figurines, thin running legs
cracked and mended, line of glossy residue,
glue made of bone.

Watching figures stalk the fields,
small flames threatening to touch off
the chaff, my brother vowed to build a barn
to hide deer during hunting season—
an old story we tell to watch him flush.
He'd seen trophies in the basements of men,
black noses giving a wet illusion.

On highways, the inside out
of a deer—viscera slick, shocking
as a stranger's nude body.
Yesterday, he said soldiers in Iraq
call tattoos *meat tags*—hard
glint in his eyes.

Fisherman

I read that fishermen
lose fingers if rings catch in netting,
and rarely do they wear wedding bands.
You're the only man I know
who could handle life
on a fishing boat, so the hand I saw
holding the net was yours.
I don't always want to be
your wife, can't make you dance
in public, don't want to give up
everyone I could love, but I confess
that when I saw you, rain slick,
red face and a rough
sea behind you, my first thought
was *how do I get him off that boat*
and home, safe beside me?

Apart

We kissed in a broken elevator
in a bar in downtown Tacoma; an elevator
stalled in the basement. We slipped inside
this metaphor and kissed
until my face felt raw.

When we returned
to Minnesota, I started
sleeping in the back bedroom, away
from our bed.

You came in the first night
and drew the curtains—*these windows
face east,* you said.

The second night you carried an extra blanket.

On the third night, you found me wrapped
in a towel, stepped in close, drank
from my collarbone. As if I were
a flower holding water in its throat,
a thing patient with drought
and cold. You touched me
like it was nothing—

nearly nothing,
that mouth on that skin.
Like tracing a circle on your own hand
again and again until it hurts.
Until you don't know
if you are touched
or doing the touching.

Split

He kneels,
hand on my sternum.

I forget how soft you are, he says.
After two days, I forget.

To preserve—
the inclination to.

If I could have,
I would've slipped away

on thin legs, become
invisible at the tree line.

I wanted. I wanted to go on
wanting. Is it any different

than any animal want,
to go on breathing

in order to love someone?

Nobody wants their life
to become unrecognizable to them.

Lost

Weeks after the last time, she bled.
It was startling. There would never be anyone
made from the way he needed her.

Montana

You and I are sitting in the sun eating ice cream with huckleberries outside the entrance to Glacier National Park. I'm wearing my white bikini top and blue jeans and I've recently cut off my long hair. Your pockets are full of blue-green stones we stole from the Kootenai River. As I eat the ice cream, I save the huckleberries under my tongue. I'm not used to you kissing me, so when you lean over, my mouth is already full of huckleberries. I'll save everything from this trip—the receipt for our admission into the park, the cork from the bottle of wine that night, the map of the campground where the ranger marked our site with a red circle.

Later that night, after the wine is gone, we lie on our backs, away from the fire, and look at the stars. When you first see them you say, *I can barely breathe.* It's so dark we can see every one—blue, orange, white—and I talk about temperature, the length of my body grazing the edge of yours. I wish you'd have brought it up, how those stars had been dead for millions of years, so it wouldn't have been such a surprise, later—what happened to you and me.

I was the one you loved first and best; the owner of a dozen names you'd chosen. My body had taken the years it needed to make itself over as something only you had touched. But it didn't matter anymore if I was dying, or if I was brilliant, or if I was lit up with a light anyone could see for miles. That last night, you knew it, even though I didn't yet. What burns has to burn itself out. I was already someone else.

$$S = k \cdot \log W$$

(Entropy, 2006)

when he enters
inside everything
fingers split
her:
yields
pressed she was
gave off
hand weighted
interminable softness
the universe was
dying stars
throat holding wine
more
despite absence
I want to give you
conifer
river's water
swallowing
ink under skin
inside warmth
dark pressure
pushing
this the place
withdraw
the heart
gives way
so far away

smell of his breath
burned sugar
an orange
what can I give you
pound of flesh
capable
scent
gift giving
yellow light
steam
a gift she said
mouthful of
more
desired effects
origins of:
exposed root
drunk
huckleberry stripped
the universe exposed
inside
heat's infancy
finger until knuckle
bone as remainder
beat/pound
then reminder:
everything
from here

there it is
skin of the wrist
remembers
she wants to give
precious
as in: grasp/hold
love–in–idleness
both breasts
a giveaway
submerged explosion
sinking
mountain air
won't yield
split and still
mourn&remember
sucking
dark pupils
branches
warmth
its core
spread across
glowing coal
carbon knocking
dispensing with
a revolving world
having moved
to where it started

III

Want

When I was twelve, I wanted a macaw
        but they cost hundreds of dollars.

If we win the lottery? I asked.
        Macaws weren't known to be great talkers,

but they were affectionate.
        Yes, my mother said. *If we win the lottery.*

I was satisfied, so long as it wasn't impossible.

The macaw would be blue.

A Poem about Childhood

A girl at Penny's was crying—
her parents wouldn't buy
the pajamas she wanted.
You didn't like them,
but you chose them, made sure
she saw when you put them in
your cart.

The pajamas were yellow;
you wore them all summer.

Dear Gretel,

Did you spend the night
curled close to his cage?
Near enough that you smelled
the straw of his bedding, did you lie there
and listen to him exhale? Did he talk
in his sleep, a sound loud, nonsensical,
its echo disappearing into dark
like a rock tossed down a well?
How did you keep him safe?
Was it merely proximity? Say the danger
is too large to fit in an oven.
What would you do?

◇◇◇

Dear Gretel,
Was it your idea to give the witch
something to pinch? The chicken bone,
I mean. Did it haunt you how akin
it was to his little finger?

◇◇◇

Dear Gretel,
They say you stole her glasses,
ground their lenses to dust, to flour.
Is that a hint? What's to steal
when hazard has excellent sight?

◇◇◇

Dear Gretel,
Did you ever consider
the moment his face
could disappear behind flames?
Did you wonder if it would be
a clear day, a Wednesday,
laundry day? That without him
you would no longer be
a sister, just a girl
with an ashy apron?

◇◇◇

Gretel,
When the stones in the pit were cold,
the witch out collecting
herbs or busy snoozing,
did you fill these lulls
with distraction? Did it help
to give him *things,* chocolate,
gummi bears, magazines
to read? If he asked for sheets
with a higher thread count or
for grass to plant,
because he was lonely
with all that dry straw,
did that finally break your heart?

◇◇◇

Gretel,
How did it feel, later,
to walk in the woods with him,
a witch's smoldering bones
just color in the sky? Was it relief you breathed,
or did you keep your fear, introduce it
to thin ice, unstable rock,
opaque water. Did you always wince,
afterward, watching him dive?

Did you let it go on too long?

For my brother, 1st Lieutenant Greg Rueth

Lament with Red Wall and Olive Tree

—After Lorca

It occurs to me the places
where the bullets entered and
escaped, and the cup
of your skull emptying of light
and filling, hourglass slow with clay,
your teeth in your mouth
and nothing left to chew.
Your last words, written
without the sway
of your duende, its pied
cloak swelling in the coil
of wind raging from the place slashed
between here and there, the figure
born of watching bulls coughing froth.
Ghastly, your last written words—*Father,*
please give this man
a donation of 1000 pesetas
for the Army. A sum
he swiftly paid, not knowing
you were already gone.
        There are men in my family
who've gone to war,
they killed other men,
men who didn't want to die—
this isn't about war, only grief.
        O, let us be birds together,
let us both be lilies *let us*
eat the ineffable bliss of having stamens
and pistils. I know a child
who replaced his father
with apples, carries
green apples, and his mother
swaps them when they soften

40

and weep sugar, waits
until he sleeps, then sets
a glossy new fruit
near his pillow.
Why apples?
Why green
apples?

About Suffering

About suffering they were never wrong, / The Old Masters . . .
                                        AUDEN

In the Chauvet caves they discovered paintings: muzzles of lions, curled lips of cave bears, shuddering flanks of mammoth and ibex. They also found human remains: skulls, knitted in places with crusts of new growth—a body, mended. When someone suffered, another fed them, brought water, kept them warm.

Thirty thousand years later, there are still corners untidy with fragments of a child's skull. Some children are carried through the street by men with eyes like beauty turned backward. The uncles of the dead children, of Suhaib and Muhammad, bear their bodies through the street. A line of men form a funeral procession to the mosque. At the back of the line: fists punch and open hands claw air, mouths open in the vowels of rage: "E," sometimes "O." But the men who carry the children are weeping. Six thousand miles away, we can see the faces of these men, and of the children. Noted are the graceful eyebrows on the ashen foreheads, the careful knots of their white shrouds.

Auden was wrong, unless all he meant was that the world is big, and there are so many places for grief to live that we can't note each address. But it's few who can turn away, leisurely, from disaster. We don't just get on with it, though we all learn, eventually, that things can kill and then turn quiet again: empty weapons and men who've fallen asleep.

Childhood

Sometimes I feel you close—
as if you're asleep on my prairie,
recreating childhood
as something durable
we could live inside:
plates of leaves, sachets
of green walnut, jar
of mud for bee stings, chain
of flowers to bless the door.

Like you, I was never fond
of growing up. I was dragged into it
by my hair, kicking, a knot
like a bird's egg on my scalp.

Listen. We could take back
your puppet theater, my lost dolls,
your small guitar, and my broken horses—
place something self-made
and frightening in the root
cellar, its floor you'd say
was the color of blood,
of the relentless reunion
of iron and iron.

An Orange

I wasn't hungry, but took down a saucepan. I wanted to see discs of yellow that butter made on milk, like when Dad made macaroni for dinner. Those little circles of light. I watched the water come to a boil. I didn't care how long it took. While I waited, I thought about how good it would feel to believe in god. To believe that benevolence took a shape; that something larger than X was out there, and it loved me. That the frozen spring, my wet socks, and empty bed were part of a plan. The Big Bang happened 13.8 billion years ago. Humans have trouble with their backs because we haven't been upright very long. We've had culture and language for 50,000 years, but our modern concept of consciousness comes from philosophers working in the 1700s.

I know that I'm missing something. It's like looking at a painting with my nose pressed against it. I have a memory of sitting on the counter when I was five, waiting while my dad peeled an orange for me. He removed all the pulp, so when he handed it to me it was the soft color of the sky in the field across the street at dusk. It glowed in his hands like a nightlight. I hadn't seen a peeled orange look like that until I saw one in a still life. The love the artist must have had for the orange, or for his paint—something was beloved. When I was five, my father never once looked at me and imagined I would be alone.

I cooked the macaroni, carried it to my table. One bite and I knew I'd over-salted it. I had to throw it away. This last part is not a metaphor. It's just what happened when I tried to make myself something to eat. But then I couldn't stop thinking about what else my dad cooked when I was little. The roux with white pepper over canned peas, the pots of chili with whole tomatoes and the chicken a la king over toast. I couldn't stop thinking that the universe is a big place, and that it's getting bigger all the time; there are hundreds of billions of stars in our galaxy and hundreds of billions of galaxies in the observable universe. In the early part of the eighteenth century, Pascal said, "The eternal silence of endless space terrifies me." It can't be true that I'm far more concerned with the emptiness of the room I'm sitting in, but somehow, I am. Somehow it's true that there was a moment in time (ten to the negative thirty-second power seconds after the Big Bang) when the entire universe was the size of an orange.

Why Loneliness

Loneliness is the first thing which God's eye named, not good.
MILTON

To make a red coat inconspicuous on a morning walk.

To ensure our notice of the heron, hovering like a kite.

To give the dry violet on the windowsill the faith she will be watered.

So that the city herself might have friends.

So that we might identify with fish that prefer shallow water.

So that we can say *feather* with thumb and forefinger. Can say *theory*.

To give us time to contemplate movement: Ana, Kata.

So that we would each wish to be lovely.

To give the moon many histories:

Ch'ang-O once slept with Jade Rabbit curled inside her sleeve.

For Edward Hopper's palate.

For to contemplate the horizon line.

For to fill in maps before anyone had struck out into nothingness.

To keep us from feeling guilt, plundering hives for honey.

To ensure the translation of the Egyptian Pyramid Texts:

Your bones are those of female hawks. You will climb down ropes of brass.

So that we might be students of the shape.

So that the powerful might have a punishment.

To understand the significance of facts:

Within twenty-one feet, a knife is deadlier than a gun.

So that everyone will not cry out at once and rupture the sky.

To ensure peace of mind: All three apples belong to you. Both fish. Every mouthful.

So that a cat might truly be admired: *For he is the quickest to his mark of any creature.*

So that some of us would learn to take charcoal and make a throat. To make ears of bronze.

So that the whole world will never be enough. For the flag shuddering at the North Pole.

For another, tranquil on the moon.

IV

What I've Learned about Cottonwoods

(I)

The body has deep fissures.
It doesn't dry well. It rots,
splits poorly—

(II)

Cottonwood is a *riparian* tree,
which pertains to rivers. The word *arrive*
originally meant *to touch the shore* as in a boat
onto the bank of a river. It's too late to tell you,
but I think you'd have liked to know—

(III)

A cottonwood's heart-shaped leaves
are the favored food of the larva
of Banded Wooly Bears. Hatching in autumn,
they spend the winter frozen.
First its heart stops, then its gut freezes,
then its blood. Were you ever listening?
I want you to listen now.

(IV)

A cottonwood's serrated leaves
split wind from light. We lie
in our bedroom shaped
like a boxcar and listen
to the cottonwood's
absentminded
rending.

(V)

The white tufts. A small child comes
into the yard, touches them, tentatively.
I think about touching our own child that way.
Imagine us, making something new in our old world.
Something that leaves a print. In Italy, they call them
flowers of the people. In Minnesota, children
pretend they're snow.

(VI)

Paste a leaf of cottonwood
on each temple and wait until it falls
on its accord, you will be cured. The word
accord comes from Latin and meant
to bring heart to heart.

(VII)

When the wind stopped, I walked into the park
to see about the cottonwood. The leaves
were torn and scattered. Fresh leaves
steeped in cold, believed to purify the blood,
to heal an inflamed heart. Upside down
against wet grass, they were the wrong
kind of green. The tree itself
was unmoved.

Boy

Last night the phone rang.
My brother said, *Afghanistan. December.*
He hadn't begun to tell us about Iraq yet.
Let's not dwell on it, he said,
meaning Afghanistan.

My brother sent pictures last year,
from Iraq—mostly of himself
petting stray dogs, though in one photo
his eye looks bruised.

I had to accept: a weapon moves
through another country
on the back of my brother,
whose head is full of glum
love songs.

It wasn't just the heat, it was
the aridity. *I'm trying to plant some grass,*
he said. *Something green.* We sent it
across the ocean as seeds. *It's so
dry here,* he said. *I can't explain.*

As kids, we spent summers
in lakes, in rivers, in pools.
My brother was first to dive,
no matter how cold the water.
No one flinched if it took time
for him to surface. We trusted
his body's ascension,
that before long, we'd see
his ecstatic face.

Styx

(I)

It's hard to forget what you're built to remember.
The river in August—doe's weathered vertebrae,

fish's white pin ribs, broken rock and rust, oily
sand—a silver heron I want to scare into flight.

Dark comes. Humidity carrying its plug
of carcass and refuse. I'm looking for the right

words but you're already far away, barely turning
to mark my progress through debris,

grit of you inside me as the heron departs.
I can't help but think of blue herons in Como Park,

our old apartment so close to this river—
what it's like to be dead. Separated

from all you once loved.

(II)

A paddlewheel shutters past—yellow lit mirage, ferry
to the spirit world. I've got an urge to swim out,

to call for help, but I photograph you instead. I take a picture
of your back. You appear just as you are. A dark shape—

(III)

On the way here, I notice your car has a sickly
sweet, interior smell like something rotting,

and the woman's sunglasses in the cup holder
you haven't bothered to remove.

(IV)

I'm picking my way over rock that clatters
like bone china and slides into water, I'm seeing

on the bank how, over time, even metal can be warped.
That even brick can be crushed—I'm so afraid, so just hold me

or drown me, please do something—

(V)

You deposit me curbside, your new habit
of not asking where I want to go, or when,

so it startles me when you put your face to my throat, say *I just
love you,* say *I just love you so much*. The two of us, we belong

back in the dark and reek, like the pair of bullheads
we found tonight, in a plastic bucket, abandoned.

Translation

—After Lorca

It's been a long night.
You keep finding a way
to speak to me. I'm weary,
from the root of the
root of me, my bees
breaking open and the lust
in the furious snap
of the flag flown over the country
of one woman.

You translate
cicada speech like something
ratcheted, tuned, and in the morning
the scratch of a stick being dragged
through sand.

How often am I the one missing
from conversations, however
patient you are with me?

You possess every word
to set anguish like a bone,
to fix it—

every word awake.
You've got all the words
though I go on, fumbling.

Let me learn another language.

Red

For weeks, flakes of eraser, curls of wood
and pigment across the landscape
of our dining room table. Poppy,
Scarlet, Carmine—

Purity of color, I learned, is ensured by the absence of iron.

I'd gotten used to the sound of pencils
rolling across the table, tapping against
the floor. The curd of white eraser,
your lovely muscled back, sore from work,
bent over the drawing of the cardinal.
The hours you spent on a single eye.

Absence makes the heart
a) grow fonder
b) go to ground

Talking to another woman late at night, you show her
the drawing, and she marvels at it, at you. You tell her
that this drawing was commissioned and will be paired with
a poem.

Not my poem, just
a poem.

If you want to see a red bird, / learn winter.

My flush of blood. My rushing heart.
Everything slipping out of place.
The rest of the body cold, heart having
gathered all blood and forced it across the face.

"An explanation [for blushing . . .] proposes that when
we feel shame we communicate our emotion to others and
in doing so we send an important signal to them. It tells
them something about us. It shows that we recognize that
something is out of place. It shows that we are sorry about
this. It shows that we want to put things right."

I used to live in Como, you told her. Now
I live in Powderhorn.

Males sometimes bring nest material to the female, [but
it's she] who does most of the building.

I called from Chicago while you were still working on
the drawing. *I wish you were here to encourage me,* you say.
This bird looks like shit now. When I say goodnight at the hotel,
you say, *I don't believe you miss me.* I don't mention the song
at the restaurant, how I had to excuse myself, how I sat and wept
in the restroom where the song was more audible.

A cardinal's call is recognized as purdy purdy purdy . . .
what-cheer what-cheer.

You bring home raspberries in chocolate pastry
shells. Bring home snap peas and flowers. I wash
work clothes, fold and leave tidy stacks on your
dresser. Pants that look as filthy out of the dryer
as they did lying on the floor. Dirty shirts with white
lines across the belly—salt your body lost in the heat.
I pack coolers with frozen washcloths, with watermelon.
I don't fold your socks the way you like. But
I bring home pineapples; I stand them upside down
to make them sweet. At night we still search for each other
across the open space of the mattress.

Cardinals are songbirds and the male uses its call to
attract a mate. Unlike most northern songbirds, the female
also sings. Females will often sing from the nest in what
may be a call to her mate.

One night you wonder at how our neighborhood in Minneapolis
can be so silent. As soon as the words exist, an ambulance's
red siren. And then our laughs; yours and mine
together make a particular sound.

> Both male and female cardinals sing clear, slurred whistled
> phrases that are vocabulary of several phrase types which
> combine into different songs.

Hour three of an argument, I say,
*Don't you have anything
to say?* Weeks later, in bed, after
I think you're asleep you say,
I don't want to lose you.

> A mated pair of cardinals shares song phrases, but the
> female may sing a longer and slightly more complex song
> than the male.

For weeks I watched you, riveted. Loved
to watch you do something I couldn't.
What you created with five pencils: black,
and white but mostly
Poppy, Scarlet, Carmine—

> It has also been suggested that blushing and flushing are
> the visible manifestations of the physiological rebound of
> the basic instinctual fight/flight mechanism, when physical
> action is not possible. The common call in a situation of
> alarm is a metallic chirp.

Let the sky be bright with all you can't see.

> *Let yourself be hungry, the world
> frayed and turning its face away in sleep.*

Let's get together, she says. She says, *Don't
be a stranger . . .*

> *[Cardinals] are obsessed with defending their territory
> against intruders. Birds may spend hours fighting these
> intruders without giving up . . . one female kept up this
> behavior every day or so for six months without stopping.*

See you soon, you say.

> *A berry splitting / with its own water.*

The next day you call and leave a message: *I just read
your cardinal poem again. It's perfect.*

> *A wound / stitching itself together.*

I watch you pack your pencils in their black case. It makes
me sad, to watch you put them away. The next day I remove
the photo of us—our first vacation in Montana—and shove it
under the dresser where I won't have to see.

> *Pairs may stay together throughout winter, but up to
> twenty percent of pairs split up by the next season.*

When you were out of town,
I sat down and arranged your colored pencils
based on a color wheel you'd taught me.
I did it because something was out of place.
I wanted to put things right.
The pencils were dull, smooth like the tips of fingers.
I sharpened every single pencil, the first knuckle
of my middle finger, raw and shining. Red.

Sketch for an Ode or Elegy

1   Not silent exactly, with the rain-stick sound of squirrels along branches; pollen from spruce trees disturbed and floating like gold smoke; even lighter than what's invisible. Sometimes I want to be

2   The cottonwood's shade protecting us from certain truths. How he woke in Japan with shards of tooth under his tongue. How my grief is nothing here; a bird's exhalation. He thinks one person's suffering can't be compared, but I love him, know who's story I would amend, if only

3   A heron floats past, then a cormorant. The sound of geese, hissing nearby. A man with a gold tooth walks to the edge of my blanket. *What do you think that means?* he asks, pointing to a faded red ribbon tied around a slender limb of a nearby catalpa tree. I don't know

4   It's time to start admitting it: misery made me beautiful. It lasted only as long as I was miserable

5   Now I'm myself again, made ordinary by love. Full fat milk steamed by favorite baristas and drawings in the mail from Nola—my smile extending past the edge of my face. Also green spines of fantasy novels, the dog and I sleeping in, X's love letters thrown in the trash with the coffee grounds. Phone calls from the friend, en route to Boston to begin her own new life. Another friend assuring, *Whatever you need, pal. Whatever you need* . . . The way my father held me close, then

6   The dog's gold face turned white in the span of one year, and I hated X for it. I had to concede

7   It's time to start brushing my hair again. The loveliest man has sat down beside me and opened a book. *You don't mind if I sit here?* He has quarters stacked beside his cup for refills. I smile; I've got all day too. *What are you reading?* Beautiful arms. Wrists. I'm a match with nothing to strike against

8   I'm still going on about loss. At the café, Khosrow says, *You should pray to the Blessed Virgin Mary. Think what she saw, and still she survived.* She wears cold blue silk, hot white light, her heart outside her body.

The Offering

No one knows what to call rapture as it builds,
      as water working itself to a boil

cannot be said to be boiling. We've no word
      for the moment before rapture—

focused on the approach we never notice
      the shape it takes

without its wings—ravenous, fragile.
      Unable to flee—pinioned

to the moment. You arrive at my altar
      with no idea

what it means to worship—to adore.
      You haven't even learned it:

ecstasy and suffering
      make the same face.

A Cold Front

It's true there were nights when I didn't sleep, with you gone out west.

You sent photos—eyelashes crusted with ice. I ate nothing but vinegar and oil on bread for weeks. I lay on the living room floor, counting all the doors in my childhood home, and still found myself awake when the room filled with light.

The trucks ran all night or they wouldn't start in the morning. Locals couldn't believe you were shingling roofs in that wind. Ice glossed your pants to your boots. The boss was tucked away back home, climate controlled, but raged about deadlines. Lost jobs. Lots of men who wanted work.

January and no place to go, bitterest month in memory—when I laid about the house and watched the dark move from one room to the next, like sealing the lid on a jar, me inside—larval, needy.

We were new in town and I hadn't realized yet how bad things were going to get for us. That month I walked alone, at Como Zoo. The lions seemed submerged in artificial light, like fish in a tank. The kudu, backdropped by cinderblocks, chewed their cud and cupped their ears toward every sound. Prey animals, an eye on each side of the head. None of us was convinced summer would come back and save us. None except the bison, their noses steaming under festival costumes of snow.

At last you came home—dirt mashed into the fibers of your clothing, the blues of your coat and sweatshirt seemed almost blanched by cold. Your face was chapped, your hands skinned and too sore to open a jar for me. Your name was misspelled on the paycheck, your per diems missing. You smelled like diesel. I felt like I was touching a stranger. Plows rumbled past. The neighbor came dashing up the stairs—our car had just been towed. A few blocks away, a lion chuffed in his sleep. On the muted television, the weatherman was gesticulating grandly toward the west.

V

Ode to a Man in Dress Clothes

When I see a man

in a dress shirt, I want

to walk up behind him,

place my hand

between his shoulders,

to rest it there

for a moment. I think

about his socks, how

he chose one pair

that morning and the rest

are still at home

in a drawer.

And his shoes—

God, those shoes, they break me,

especially when they're polished, what

does he do to make them shine

like that, yes, all it takes

is a pair of shiny black shoes and such

a wave of tenderness

collapses over me

that I see his ties, at rest

on their little carousel, imagine

that he held them up

in the mirror

at the department store,

unsure.

Figure Drawing

On the way to your studio, a Cooper's hawk
dove in front of me. It left clutching yellow leaves
and not a single sparrow. I knew then,
somehow, that I would never take my own life.
And I knew it when I sat still
before your easel and watched you
holding your sighting stick to measure
my trunk. Occasionally, you pressed fingers
against my legs and hips, bluntly
but with care. You are learning
about the body and its trappings.
You've referred to my clavicle as a bony
landmark. There are so many ways to speak
about the body. There is a mundane history
of people telling their god, *If you'd asked me*
if I wanted to come here, I would have said no.
When I was your age, I entered the woods
with my hurt and sat against a tree and was
surrounded by deer that paid me no mind.
Their feet made no noise. They had no scent,
no color. You've painted my hair across my back
as fire. You've painted my face in mourning
and didn't know. Sometimes I'm filled with fear
at the thought of seeing this through,
like I was that day in the woods, when all I wanted
was to lie like a dropped antler on the forest floor.
Still, today I'm thrilled to be shown
the muscles of my own back, drawn in charcoal.
The bones of my pelvis seem larger than my hips,
warmed over with skin. We've a history of telling our gods,
If you asked me if I wanted to leave here,
I would say no. Done with your work, we walk
to the diner for pancakes. You have a smudge
of yolk-colored pigment under your nose,
another ashy smudge near your right ear.

I know how easily I could have missed it.
Whatever else happens, I don't want to miss it.
The machine of my body is humming. There is a record
of my body, resting on your easel. It is static, almost.
I saw the Cooper's hawk leave the ground with nothing,
and carry it into the air. The nothing he carried
was yellow. It was the most beautiful thing.

Despite

Despite fear, which is alive and breathes in me and turns
three times attempting to lie down. Despite my body
that burns along its vagus nerve and is ninety percent gut.
Despite this body that is crushed like a corsage
against the chest of the one I love. Despite my mind,
which wants to tell the whole truth—forgets
it's honest to say: *the body I'm trapped inside has a thorax*
and a compound eye. Despite the way I can love
anyone at all; the stranger in the courtyard—her one bare foot
dangling over the edge of a low stone wall—despite my desire
to hold the elegant arch of her. Despite pulled hair,
disturbed sleep, bent flatware—despite memory's
clean scent. Despite all blood, the realities of brain
as tissue like any other soft matter, and despite
the possibility that all we are is flesh. Despite the only sealed door
I batter myself against, and my naked body, my empty
body. Despite all the ways a body can be empty.
Despite the eagle's four-hundred-pounds-per-square-inch
grip and the whip width of her tether. Despite the way she screamed,
watching a bird outside fly the river's length. Despite the dog,
moldering, how I grieve her white eyelashes, her quick gusts
of breath when she dreamed or ran. Despite what we've been taking
for granted: first among them, the blood still inside our bodies.
Despite the dead god of my youth who promised his protection,
who smelled like dust and tasted like starch and sounded like a sudden
bell. Despite his evaporation. Despite the fact that I don't know
how I got here but still belong in this place. Despite the fragility
of our eyes, the liquid that holds light, our thin skulls, our fingernails growing
at the same rate at which the moon leaves the earth behind,
and the possibility that all we are is flesh. Despite the lasso of color—
the aura and the sting. Despite the dishes that need to be done,
the sheets we dirtied that I continue to sleep in. Despite the fruitless search
for a single piece of important paper, the simple economics
of my even simpler wealth. Despite inadequate technologies.

The matchless touch. Exhaustion. Despite the miles between us
and how the universe has labeled us a Roman candle.
Despite how we eject stars, how we're not even a slow burn,
nothing like a standing stone.

Deer through a Boutique Window

Some things can't be mended.
Some of us are broken, and some
remain whole. Something has died
in every place on earth. But I can't stop
thinking about hooves on waxed, black diamonds
of linoleum—also thousands of deer,
unharmed in the woods, bedding down,
and fawns unborn to this doe, wrecked
among silk stockings, satin slips, pearl
earrings. How do we get lost in such a small world?
Why are some of us lucky? And some of us
not? There she lies, scent of her own blood
in her nose, the elegant pheromones
in their frosted glass bottles, oblivious,
unbroken on the shelf.

Song for the Festival

At the May Day parade, my mask made of moss
and bark, my hair full of flowers, my friend beside me,
her pretty red mouth under the hawk's beak
of her mask of green sage.

At the children's pageant, music
died in the speakers. The shadow
of a crow passed over. My hair a crown
of flowers, yellow and red roses large as fists,
flowers on which I'd spent my last $20
at the mercado.

But beauty wasn't enough. Being admired
by strangers was not enough.

I saw a girl, wandering, looking for her mother.
I knelt down, lowered my mask, showed her
my face. *She's looking for you too,* I say.
She tries to spot her mother's yellow dress.
A gold dog passes, happy and white-faced,
wearing pink nylon fairy wings. The girl points
and laughs; the hard part of her day
is over.

The people I'm looking for—I don't know where they are.
I don't know the color of their clothing. From across the park,
I see the dark windows of my apartment.

Spring has arrived.
Let me not despair.

Mule Trail

Stirring the fire's coals with a stick—a familiar sound
I couldn't place until I shut my eyes—
the sound of walking through snow.

Each morning now, I wake thinking of him
because all night I hold on—like at the motel
when I slept curled around him, back against the headboard,

my hands in his gold hair. I'm trying to find a place to rest,
but loving him is like flying, like being starlings,
knowing when to move and how. It's nothing

like migration; no safe landings in brackish,
green estuaries. Still, there's the way the match hisses
when I touch its head to the glass of water.

There's the way he loves me. There's the way
the sun can heat the juice inside a berry
to the temperature of blood, and how good he is

at loving me. Something is building inside.
Pearls make me think of fevers. Blood oranges,
finches, the stick of a fish's silver skin to its flesh—

what do you do, when you realize you want
the whole of everything inside of you?
I don't want to tell what I've learned—

there's no way to repel love or to draw it close.
I don't want to say I'm bewildered, but
what makes a man love a woman?

I know the way he loves is not for spectacle. I know
this will not last. Before the end we'll drive to the desert
to see it bloom, to see vacant motels and red-gold buttes,

see the desert's blue stars and the collapsing
castles of its abandoned mini-golf courses,
the dark signs of its empty diners.

For now we have Mule Trail, where everything
looks like something else. The firewood in the pit,
lit from inside like a church's stained-glass window,

the plum's gold flesh laced with scarlet veins,
replica of a human brain. Maybe this is all we are—
carbon, water, color. We spent the storm in the tent,

woke up later and rebuilt the fire, heard coyotes'
eerie chatter, then the wolves'—lower and wiser,
with authority. Why am I so ungainly with love

after all the loving I've done? I didn't realize
until I was hours away—the insect bites, the pin-sized
blisters of stinging nettle, the raw interior skin.

What does it mean to be in love? As it turns out,
the second best thing that can happen to you
is a broken heart.

Two Trains

Two trains leave different cities heading toward each other at different speeds. When the man in train #1 slides across the seat to kiss the woman who has been looking out the window, what texture is the upholstery of the seat on that train if the upholstery in train #2 is a faded, tobacco-colored naugahyde? If the conductor of train #2 had not had to milk the cows every morning and afternoon of his childhood, would he have had more time to stay after school, peering in microscopes? In this case, who would then be commanding train #2? If the conductor of train #1 was able to express how much he loved to drive the train into the night, that he imagined it, not along any track, just shoving into the dark, never arriving to bathe in the bright lights of Seattle, would they demote him to porter? If the porter in train #1 was not pretending to be well when in fact he was sick, who would care for him? Which city? Which woman: the one with the salmon-colored geraniums, or the one whose stockings drip all night against the radiator? When the man in train #2 drops his briefcase, and it pops open, sending seven small bottles to bounce soundlessly across the carpeted aisle, will the small girl who witnessed it remember the color of the bottles later? Will she think of them when she sees, for the first time, the sulfuric green water, on her honeymoon, in Yellowstone National Park? Who is her spouse? Which train have they boarded? When and where do they meet?

May Day

I've lived in my neighborhood long enough to recognize
that morning glories bloom early here—they don't signify the end
of summer. I'm beginning to understand that parts of me
are wasted entirely.

Somewhere it's the last snow of April and the dead dog knows.
Somewhere my lost uncle is eating sweet and sour at Ming's, steam
touching his face so gently.

If something happens in this world, it goes on
for billions of years, but if something doesn't happen, it never does.
For a billion years I rock the babies of other women.

Tell me I've nothing to fear.

Powderhorn, after the Storm

It's vertigo, walking among downed trees'
belled skirts of dirt and tender clover.
Birds sit on branches laid prone
over fragrant hearts of trunks.
Hearts slick and white. So many trees
uprooted, yet some bushes kept
pink blossoms, which today are open,
tender throats. My dogs and I traverse
the wounds, full of heady bliss,
as when a fever breaks
or morphine is administered—
there's a suppleness to everything.
A dampness. One of the dogs bounds
through debris, the other picks
her way. Both are old. Neither
seems to realize it, though one
is suddenly afraid of thunder,
has spent the last two nights
whining at my bedside
and pissing on the floor.
I lost my temper
when I took her out at 3 a.m.,
fingers of sirens reaching
from all directions, hazard
lights of crushed cars blinking
an anxious orange in the dark.
I jerked her leash, nudged
her through the door
with my knee. These cruelties
aren't held against me.
I regret them deeply.
Now there's light from another,
better world. The sun is out.
We stop at the water fountain
and I cup my hands to give them a drink.

The tentative dog, the one who was afraid
and who I betrayed, drinks from my hands.
Her gentle mouth and soft tongue.
I fill my hands for her
again and again.

What We Will Love with the Time We Have Left

All life will die, all mind will cease, and it will all be as if it never happened. That, to be honest, is the goal to which evolution is traveling, that is the "benevolent" end of the furious living and furious dying . . . All life is no more than a match struck in the dark and blown out again. The final result . . . is to deprive it completely of meaning.

LESLIE PAUL

First, the purple flowers growing along the sidewalk,
so saturated with color they make us blind to look at them.
Then, the sound of a screen door slamming, the smell of pine pollen
and beeswax. The silvery eyes of the concrete deer, guarding
a bird bath. The uncomfortable feel of wet jeans, stiff with sand.
The taste of well water from an aluminum cup. The sound of water
being poured into a glass. Hot tea with one ice cube in it.
The silk of frog skin and the stinging nettle. Smell of wet rock. Scent
of aftershave on steam. Squeak of finger against the mirror.
The day-old cookies in their white paper bag, brought home
to surprise the dogs. The lambswool way an old dog's legs feel,
her body failing her. The way the child sings a song
she was taught about loneliness, before being taught
about loneliness. Throats, armpits, arches of feet. Perfunctory
head nods of strangers walking the opposite direction. The smoke
pulled in soft, through the open window along with the wind
through wet hair. The twin images of neurons and cluster galaxies. The cold
calm of a museum exhibit—maces and daggers, backlit and serene.
The way Bernini made marble supple, the way Caravaggio's brutal
hands painted light. All the furious living, the turtle dragging herself, algaed
from the lake to the sand at the top of the playground to lay her eggs. All the furious
dying. The unidentifiable viscera that the wasps are drinking from
on the sidewalk. The way the wasps relish it. The heron lifting off
with the skyline behind her. Berries, crushed in mouths. The alabaster egg.
The toy horse. The little brother at age three, in his gray pajamas, waving.
The light and heat of the fairgrounds, the airy relief of the gondola in its primary
colors and the dank cool of the dark mill ride. The warm hand, and the water lapping
against the side of the boat. Even the memory of them. The sulfur
of a match struck, the dark it removes and the way the dark comes back.

Acknowledgments

Thank you to the editors of the following magazines and journals, where these poems originally appeared, sometimes in earlier forms. Academy of American Poets *Poem-a-Day:* "Song for the Festival." *Mas Tequila Review:* "Translation," "Gregory," and "Macrocosm/Microcosm." *Midway Journal:* "Know Me," "Fisherman," and "Split." *Paper Darts:* "Prologue" and "I Know One Thing for Sure." *The Paris Review* and *Harper's Magazine:* "Ode to a Man in Dress Clothes." *Poetry:* "Painted Turtle" and "Want." *Poetry City, USA:* "Elsewhere." *Sleet Magazine:* "A Poem about Childhood." *Tin House:* "Andromeda" and "Despite." *TriQuarterly:* "Figure Drawing." *What Light! (MNartists.org):* "Why Loneliness."

Nothing is accomplished alone, and I feel blessed with an abundance of care and support. To the following people, I express my appreciation: Deborah Keenan, Patricia Kirkpatrick, Katrina Vandenberg, Bill Meissner, Bonnie West, Sasha Ivanovsky-Schow, Paige Riehl, Elena Cisneros, Anna George Meek, Susan Solomon, Mark Anderson, Jim Blaha, Peter Campion, Krisanne Dattir, Todd Pederson, Carlee Alson, Josiah Titus, Charlie Broderick, Courtney Algeo, Anika Eide, Jamie Buehner, Tracy Mumford, Jevin Boardman, Beth Berila, Amy Boland, Siobhan DiZio, Gabrielle Rose, Sandra Evans, Mary Cassidy, Richard Jarrette, Kate Kysar, Betsy Brown, Su Smallen, Colin McDonald, Kelly Hansen Maher, Richard Brown, Lewis Mundt, Dore Kiesselbach, Ali Maki, and Susan Schaffer. Special thanks to Matt Mauch, for helping me to find the right name for this book, and to Eamonn McLain for the painting that became my cover. Thank you Jim Moore, Caitlin Bailey, Allison Wigen, and Nikki Ivanovsky-Schow, for your consistent friendship and encouragement. I have sincere gratitude for the support from my family: David, Sue, and Greg Rueth, and Zach, Bridget, and Nola Reineking. Thank you to the Loft Literary Center for their support through their Emerging Writers' Grant. Finally, an enormous thank you to Jeff Shotts, dream editor, and the rest of the team at Graywolf Press.

"Sketch for an Ode or Elegy" is for Kyle, Caitlin, and Allison
"Figure Drawing" is for Nikki

The italicized line in "Andromeda" is from Lorca's poem "Gacela del Amor Imprevisto," translated by Catherine Brown.

The italicized lines in "Lament with Red Wall and Olive Tree" are taken from Lorca's essay "Mistica de la melancolía," translated by Christopher Maurer.

The poem, "About Suffering," is in response to W. H. Auden's poem "Musée des Beaux Arts," and was inspired by Paul Hansen's photograph, which was named World Press Photo of the Year in 2013.

In the third part of "What I've Learned about Cottonwoods," the information about the hibernation of Banded Wooly Bear caterpillars is taken from *Frozen Planet,* a documentary series produced by the BBC.

Some of the text from the poem "Red" comes from Ray Crozier's essay "The Puzzle of Blushing" and from the Cornell Lab of Ornithology's guide to cardinals.

GRETCHEN MARQUETTE has published her poems in several magazines and anthologies, including *Harper's,* the *Paris Review, Poetry,* and *Tin House.* She is a recipient of a Minnesota Emerging Writers' Grant through the Loft Literary Center, and she earned her MFA in creative writing from Hamline University, where she served as assistant poetry editor for *Water~Stone Review.* Marquette lives in the Powderhorn neighborhood in south Minneapolis.

The text of *May Day* is set in Bembo.
Book design by Rachel Holscher.
Composition by Bookmobile Design & Digital Publisher Services, Minneapolis, Minnesota.
Manufactured by Versa Press on acid-free, 30 percent postconsumer wastepaper.